CROWN CLASSICS

★

JONATHAN SWIFT

A SELECTION OF POEMS

BY

JONATHAN SWIFT

EDITED

WITH AN INTRODUCTION

BY

JOHN HEATH-STUBBS

LONDON

THE GREY WALLS PRESS LTD

First published in 1948
by the Grey Walls Press Limited
7 Crown Passage, Pall Mall, London, S.W.1
Printed in Great Britain
by Waterlow and Sons Limited
London and Dunstable

CONTENTS

★

INTRODUCTION

★

THE so-called Augustan Age of English literature repre-
sents one of those rare moments in history when
perfection of style is achieved. This perfection sym-
bolizes the momentary triumph of civilization and the human
intellect over that chaos which lies eternally around and within
us. The men of the eighteenth century found themselves in a
world which had at last attained a breathing-space after the
religious and political conflicts of the preceding age, when the
forces of bigotry and fanaticism had been unloosed upon the
world. Casting their gaze farther backwards they saw the Middle
Ages only as a long night of superstition and ignorance, whose
slumbers had been broken at last by the voice of Erasmus.
Beyond that was the civilization of the ancient world: the Rome
of Augustus and Virgil, of Horace and of Maecenas—a world
in which they recognized their own counterpart and exemplar;
and, more remote, with a radiance too bright, indeed, for their
cool, reasonable understanding, was Athens. In the whole of
the rest of the landscape of human history there was little else
to be discerned but barbarism.

But now God had said, 'Let Newton be!', and all was light.
The laws of the Universe were revealed—simple, reasonable,
beautiful—mathematical laws, which exemplified the all-
embracing wisdom and foresight of the Supreme Being. Yet
though chaos seemed to have been banished, the victory was
not lightly won. The greatest geniuses of the age—Pope, its
most absolute poet, Swift himself, and later, Johnson with his
grave and profound melancholy—are acutely conscious of the
forces of unreason which continually threaten them. It is these

forces, and not really the forgotten hacks of Grub Street, who are seen marshalling behind the goddess Dullness at the end of the *Dunciad*:

> *Thy hand, great anarch! lets the curtain fall,*
> *And universal darkness buries all.*

The whole of the eighteenth century suffered from a deep-rooted spiritual anxiety. It is surely no coincidence that madness overwhelmed Swift, Collins, Smart, and Cowper and threatened Johnson and Boswell. It was something very like madness, too, which drove Pope to weave his incredible spider-webs of intrigue and deception. In a milder form, the same *malaise* was the 'white melancholy' of Gray, and that fashionable disease, 'the spleen', which Matthew Green and the Countess of Winchelsea celebrated in verse.

At the end of the century chaos was to break loose once more. It expressed itself in the Gothic extravagances of the early Romantics, in the elegant satanism of the Hell-fire Club. It took on a new creative energy in the emotional religious outbursts of the Methodist and Evangelical revivals, claiming poor Cowper as one of its casualties. Finally, in the French Revolution and the Terror, it swept aside the eighteenth-century compromise for ever.

In the work of Swift and Pope style is still strong enough to contain and limit chaos. But chaos is never far absent from their minds, and the consciousness of this gives to their work a kind of smouldering, nervous intensity, underlying its apparently calm surface. Irony is the quality in which they excel, and it is a double-edged weapon. Take, for example, Swift's *A Modest Proposal*, in which he suggests that the poor may prevent their children from becoming a burden to them by selling them as food to the rich. How much more than simple sarcasm this is! As we read Swift's cool, reasoned prose, the careful computation of the exact sum which would be saved by such a scheme, the enumeration of the various advantages

8

which would accrue to the whole community, how much do we not realize about society, and the real nature of the relations between rich and poor? Are they, stripped of our customary evasions, so different from this after all? But farther still below the surface there is a deeper and even more terrible irony. Who, reading these pages, can quite rid himself of the haunting suspicion that, deep down in his nature, Swift also shared that utter contempt for the Irish poor which by implication he imputes to his readers; and that a part of him, belonging not to the conscious intellectual self at all, but to the primeval savage which lurks in all of us, envisaged with pleasure the cannibalistic scheme which his real indignation and pity for the poor had created for itself as a satirical weapon?

The madness which finally overcame Swift was, almost certainly, of a wholly physical and organic origin—though modern psychology should make us beware of drawing too hard and fast a line between the physical and the psychological in such matters. But, in any case, it was the overturning of a mind absolutely hard, bright, and clear in its intellectual qualities. Happiness was once defined by Swift as the art of 'being well deceived'; it was that deception which all his life he refused. His intellect could not compromise with the facts of the physical world—hence his continual horror of the natural functions of the human body, its effluvia and its excrement. But the physical world, as always, had its revenge; and a bodily imbecility overthrew and blotted out that intellect in the end. In his continual dwelling on the facts of defæcation there was an obsessive quality, a perverse love. At the end of *Gulliver's Travels*, refusing to accept humanity as it is, he degrades it to the status of the Yahoos, and finds his ideal, not in something surpassing the human, but in the brute, the horse.

Swift's verse is comparatively little read, but it is, as much as his prose, the expression of his personality—the enigmatic personality of a very unhappy, very great man. It may not appeal to the lover of romantic verse, or any, perhaps, but those who have learned to appreciate a certain dry elegance which is essentially a quality of classical poetry. Like his prose, it is of the Doric order, free from all unnecessary ornament, yet with an intellectual poetic fire of its own. Swift, in the light conversational octosyllabic couplet, attained a mastery comparable to that of his friend Pope in the more formal decasyllabic. Much of his verse is occasional, even ephemeral—but the force of his satire sometimes lifts it into a kind of macabre horror, and it becomes, as in the astonishing and terrible poem *On the Death of Dr. Swift*, a veritable Dance of Death. But his characteristic tone is one of light and civilized raillery, the irony with which he strove to mask that savage indignation at life which habitually tore at his breast. *Cadenus and Vanessa* (too long, unfortunately, to be given in full in the present selection) is as perfect in its way as Pope's *Rape of the Lock*. In it, Swift strove, by disguising the affair in a framework of elaborate allegory, to wean Esther Vanhomrigh from the unfortunate passion which she had conceived for the man who had sought only to raise her to the status of an intellectual equal by the cultivation of her mind. But the poem was ineffective; poor Vanessa would not be warned, and died broken-hearted. With Stella alone, perhaps, did Swift succeed in establishing that intimate intellectual relationship which he sought. No one will ever know what was the real nature of the feeling between these two. Some have thought that they were secretly married. The Victorian sentimentalist, Thackeray, absurdly represented Swift as cold-bloodedly exploiting the tender devotion of Stella. Yeats, in his play *The Words upon the Window-pane*, makes Swift refuse to marry and beget children, because he foresees the chaos that is to come. Mr. Denis Johnston, in a brilliant radio programme, *Weep for Polyphemus*, first put forward, in 1938, the suggestion that Swift and Stella (Esther Johnson) were really uncle and niece, she being the natural daughter of Sir William Temple, and he the illegitimate son of the latter's father, Sir John; according to this hypothesis, the discovery of the presumed blood-relationship put a permanent bar to their association as lovers. But all we know is that their friendship was a lasting one. It endured for thirty-six years and was cut short only by Stella's death—a severe blow to Swift. Before he persuaded her and her companion, Mrs. Dingley, to come and live near him in Dublin, Swift corresponded regularly with them, putting down the most intimate account of his life in the *Journal to Stella*. That document remains, and with it the poems which Swift annually wrote for Stella's birthday. The latter, with their combination of unsentimental tenderness, wit, and good sense, are among his most perfect, most pleasing and most baffling productions. These two human souls keep their secret, as they move with a reserved smile in their formal dance. They refuse our questionings, and they do not require, perhaps, our pity.

JOHN HEATH-STUBBS

A SELECTION

OF POEMS

BY

JONATHAN SWIFT

*

TRUTH

from
ODE TO DR. WILLIAM SANCROFT

TRUTH is eternal, and the Son of Heaven,
Bright effluence of th' immortal ray,
Chief cherub, and chief lamp, of that high sacred Seven,
Which guard the throne by night, and are its light by day;
    First of God's darling attributes,
    Thou daily seest him face to face,
Nor does thy essence fix'd depend on giddy circumstance
    Of time or place,
Two foolish guides in every sublunary dance;
How shall we find Thee then in dark disputes?
How shall we search Thee in a battle gain'd,
Or a weak argument by force maintain'd?
In dagger contests, and th' artillery of words,
(For swords are madmen's tongues, and tongues are madmen's
      swords,)
    Contrived to tire all patience out,
    And not to satisfy the doubt?

13

But where is even thy Image on our earth?
  For of the person much I fear,
Since Heaven will claim its residence, as well as birth,
And God Himself has said, He shall not find it here.
For this inferior world is but Heaven's dusky shade,
By dark reverted rays from its reflection made;
  Whence the weak shapes wild and imperfect pass,
  Like sunbeams shot at too far distance from a glass.

BAUCIS AND PHILEMON

*On the Ever-Lamented Loss of the Two Yew-Trees in the Parish
of Chilthorne, Somerset. 1706. Imitated from the Eighth Book
of Ovid*

IN ancient times, as story tells,
The saints would often leave their cells,
And stroll about, but hide their quality,
To try good people's hospitality.

  It happen'd on a winter night,
As authors of the legend write,
Two brother hermits, saints by trade,
Taking their tour in masquerade,
Disguis'd in tatter'd habits, went
To a small village down in Kent;
Where, in the strollers' canting strain,
They begg'd from door to door in vain,
Try'd ev'ry tone might pity win;
But not a soul would let them in.

  Our wand'ring saints, in woful state,
Treated at this ungodly rate,
Having thro' all the village past,
To a small cottage came at last
Where dwelt a good old honest ye'man,

Call'd in the neighbourhood Philemon;
Who kindly did these saints invite
In his poor hut to pass the night;
And then the hospitable sire
Bid Goody Baucis mend the fire;
While he from out the chimney took
A flitch of bacon off the hook,
And freely from the fattest side
Cut out large slices to be fry'd;
Then stepp'd aside to fetch 'em drink,
Fill'd a large jug up to the brink,
And saw it fairly twice go round;
Yet (what was wonderful) they found
'Twas still replenish'd to the top,
As if they ne'er had touch'd a drop.
The good old couple were amaz'd,
And often on each other gaz'd;
For both were frighten'd to the heart,
And just began to cry, 'What *art!*'
Then softly turn'd aside, to view
Whether the lights were burning blue.
The gentle pilgrims, soon aware on't,
Told them their calling and their errand:
'Good folk, you need not be afraid,
We are but saints,' the hermits said;
'No hurt shall come to you or yours:
But for that pack of churlish boors,
Not fit to live on Christian ground,
They and their houses shall be drown'd;
While you shall see your cottage rise,
And grow a church before your eyes.'

They scarce had spoke, when fair and soft,
The roof began to mount aloft;
Aloft rose ev'ry beam and rafter;
The heavy wall climb'd slowly after.

The chimney widen'd and grew higher
Became a steeple with a spire.

The kettle to the top was hoist,
And there stood fasten'd to a joist,
But with the upside down, to show
Its inclination for below:
In vain; for a superior force
Applied at bottom stops its course:
Doom'd ever in suspense to dwell,
'Tis now no kettle, but a bell.

A wooden jack, which had almost
Lost by disuse the art to roast,
A sudden alteration feels,
Increas'd by new intestine wheels;
And, what exalts the wonder more,
The number made the motion slower.
The flyer, though it had leaden feet,
Turn'd round so quick you scarce could see't;
But, slacken'd by some secret power,
Now hardly moves an inch an hour.
The jack and chimney, near ally'd,
Had never left each other's side;
The chimney to a steeple grown,
The jack would not be left alone;
But, up against the steeple rear'd,
Became a clock, and still adher'd;
And still its love to household cares,
By a shrill voice at noon, declares,
Warning the cook-maid not to burn
That roast meat, which it cannot turn.
The groaning-chair began to crawl,
Like an huge snail, half up the wall;
There stuck aloft in public view,
And with small change, a pulpit grew.

The porringers, that in a row

Hung high, and made a glitt'ring show,
To a less noble substance chang'd,
Were now but leathern buckets rang'd.

The ballads, pasted on the wall,
Of Joan of France, and English Mall,
Fair Rosamond, and Robin Hood,
The little Children in the Wood,
Now seem'd to look abundance better,
Improved in picture, size, and letter:
And, high in order plac'd, describe
The heraldry of ev'ry tribe.

A bedstead of the antique mode,
Compact of timber many a load,
Such as our ancestors did use,
Was metamorphos'd into pews;
Which still their ancient nature keep
By lodging folk disposed to sleep.

The cottage, by such feats as these,
Grown to a church by just degrees,
The hermits then desired their host
To ask for what he fancy'd most.
Philemon, having paused a while,
Return'd them thanks in homely style;
Then said, 'My house is grown so fine,
Methinks, I still would call it mine.
I'm old, and fain would live at ease;
Make me the parson if you please.'

He spoke, and presently he feels
His grazier's coat fall down his heels:
He sees, yet hardly can believe,
About each arm a pudding sleeve;
His waistcoat to a cassock grew,
And both assumed a sable hue;
But, being old, continued just
As threadbare, and as full of dust.

B

His talk was now of tithes and dues:
Could smoke his pipe, and read the news;
Knew how to preach old sermons next,
Vamp'd in the preface and the text;
At christ'nings well could act his part,
And had the service all by heart;
Wish'd women might have children fast,
And thought whose sow had farrow'd last;
Against dissenters would repine,
And stood up firm for 'right divine';
Found his head fill'd with many a system;
But classic authors,—he ne'er mist 'em.

Thus having furbish'd up a parson,
Dame Baucis next they play'd their farce on.
Instead of homespun, coifs were seen
Good pinners edg'd with colberteen;
Her petticoat, transform'd apace,
Became black satin, flounced with lace.
'Plain Goody' would no longer down,
'Twas 'Madam', in her grogram gown.
Philemon was in great surprise,
And hardly could believe his eyes.
Amaz'd to see her look so prim,
And she admir'd as much at him.

Thus happy in their change of life,
Were several years this man and wife:
When on a day, which prov'd their last,
Discoursing o'er old stories past,
They went by chance, amidst their talk,
To the churchyard to take a walk;
When Baucis hastily cry'd out,
'My dear, I see your forehead sprout!'—
'Sprout', quoth the man, 'what's this you tell us?
I hope you don't believe me jealous!
But yet, methinks, I feel it true,

And really yours is budding too—
Nay,—now I cannot stir my foot;
It feels as if 'twere taking root.'
    Description would but tire my Muse,
In short, they both were turn'd to yews.
Old Goodman Dobson of the Green
Remembers he the trees has seen;
He'll talk of them from noon till night,
And goes with folk to show the sight;
On Sundays after evening prayer,
He gathers all the parish there;
Points out the place of either yew,
Here Baucis, there Philemon, grew:
Till once a parson of our town,
To mend his barn, cut Baucis down;
At which, 'tis hard to be believ'd,
How much the other tree was griev'd,
Grew scrubby, dy'd a-top, was stunted,
So the next parson stubb'd and burnt it.

A DESCRIPTION OF THE MORNING

Now hardly here and there an hackney-coach
Appearing, show'd the ruddy morn's approach,
Now Betty from her master's bed had flown,
And softly stole to discompose her own;
The slip-shod 'prentice from his master's door
Had pared the dirt, and sprinkled round the floor.
Now Moll had whirl'd her mop with dext'rous airs,
Prepared to scrub the entry and the stairs.
The youth with broomy stumps began to trace
The kennel's edge, where wheels had worn the place.
The small-coal man was heard with cadence deep,

Till drown'd in shriller notes of chimney-sweep;
Duns at his lordship's gate began to meet;
And brickdust Moll had scream'd through half the street.
The turnkey now his flock returning sees,
Duly let out a-nights to steal for fees:
The watchful bailiffs take their silent stands,
And schoolboys lag with satchels in their hands.

A DESCRIPTION OF A CITY SHOWER

Careful observers may foretell the hour,
(By sure prognostics,) when to dread a shower.
While rain depends, the pensive cat gives o'er
Her frolics, and pursues her tail no more.
Returning home at night, you'll find the sink
Strike your offended sense with double stink.
If you be wise, then, go not far to dine:
You'll spend in coach-hire more than save in wine.
A coming shower your shooting corns presage,
Old a–ches throb, your hollow tooth will rage;
Sauntering in coffeehouse is Dulman seen;
He damns the climate, and complains of spleen.
Meanwhile the South, rising with dabbled wings,
A sable cloud athwart the welkin flings,
That swill'd more liquor than it could contain,
And, like a drunkard, gives it up again.
Brisk Susan whips her linen from the rope,
While the first drizzling shower is borne aslope;
Such is that sprinkling which some careless quean
Flirts on you from her mop, but not so clean:
You fly, invoke the gods; then, turning, stop
To rail; she singing, still whirls on her mop.
Not yet the dust had shunn'd the unequal strife,

But, aided by the wind, fought still for life,
And wafted with its foe by violent gust,
'Twas doubtful which was rain, and which was dust.
Ah! where must needy poet seek for aid,
When dust and rain at once his coat invade?
Sole coat! where dust, cemented by the rain,
Erects the nap, and leaves a cloudy stain!
Now in contiguous drops the flood comes down,
Threatening with deluge this *devoted* town.
To shops in crowds the draggled females fly,
Pretend to cheapen goods, but nothing buy.
The Templar spruce, while every spout's abroach,
Stays till 'tis fair, yet seems to call a coach.
The tuck'd up sempstress walks with hasty strides,
While streams run down her oil'd umbrella's sides.
Here various kinds, by various fortunes led,
Commence acquaintance underneath a shed.
Triumphant Tories, and desponding Whigs,
Forget their feuds, and join to save their wigs.
Box'd in a chair the beau impatient sits,
While spouts run clattering o'er the roof by fits,
And ever and anon with frightful din
The leather sounds; he trembles from within.
So when Troy chairmen bore the wooden steed,
Pregnant with Greeks impatient to be freed,
(Those bully Greeks, who, as the moderns do,
Instead of paying chairmen, ran them through,)
Laocoön struck the outside with his spear,
And each imprison'd hero quaked for fear.
   Now from all parts the swelling kennels flow,
And bear their trophies with them as they go:
Filth of all hues and odour, seem to tell
What street they sail'd from, by their sight and smell.
They, as each torrent drives with rapid force,
From Smithfield to St. Pulchre's shape their course,

And in huge confluence join'd at Snowhill ridge,
Fall from the conduit prone to Holborn bridge.
Sweeping from butchers' stalls, dung, guts, and blood,
Drown'd puppies, stinking sprats, all drench'd in mud,
Dead cats, and turnip-tops, come tumbling down the
    flood.

PHYLLIS
OR, THE PROGRESS OF LOVE

Desponding Phyllis was endu'd
With ev'ry talent of a prude:
She trembled when a man drew near;
Salute her, and she turn'd her ear:
If o'er against her you were placed,
She durst not look above your waist:
She'd rather take you to her bed,
Than let you see her dress her head;
In church you hear her, thro' the crowd,
Repeat the absolution loud:
In church, secure behind her fan,
She durst behold that monster, man:
There practis'd how to place her head,
And bite her lips to make them red;
Or, on the mat devoutly kneeling,
Would lift her eyes up to the ceiling.
And heave her bosom unaware,
For neighb'ring beaux to see it bare.
    At length a lucky lover came,
And found admittance to the dame.
Suppose all parties now agreed,
The writings drawn, the lawyer feed,
The vicar and the ring bespoke:
Guess, how could such a match be broke?

See then what mortals place their bliss in!
Next morn betimes the bride was missing:
The mother scream'd, the father chid;
Where can this idle wench be hid?
No news of Phyl! the bridegroom came,
And thought his bride had skulk'd for shame;
Because her father used to say,
The girl had such a bashful way!

   Now John the butler must be sent
To learn the road that Phyllis went:
The groom was wish'd to saddle crop;
For John must neither light nor stop,
But find her, wheresoe'er she fled,
And bring her back, alive or dead.

   See here again the devil to do!
For truly John was missing too:
The horse and pillion both were gone!
Phyllis, it seems, was fled with John.

   Old Madam, who went up to find
What papers Phyl had left behind,
A letter on the toilet sees,
'To my much honour'd father—these—'
('Tis always done, romances tell us,
When daughters run away with fellows,)
Fill'd with the choicest common-places,
By others used in the like cases.
'That long ago a fortune-teller
Exactly said what now befell her;
And in a glass had made her see
A serving-man of low degree.
It was her fate, must be forgiven;
For marriages were made in Heaven:
His pardon begg'd: but, to be plain,
She'd do't if 'twere to do again:
Thank'd God, 'twas neither shame nor sin;

23

For John was come of honest kin.
Love never thinks of rich and poor;
She'd beg with John from door to door.
Forgive her, if it be a crime;
She'll never do't another time.
She ne'er before in all her life
Once disobey'd him, maid nor wife.'
One argument she summ'd up all in,
'The thing was done and past recalling;
And therefore hoped she could recover
His favour when his passion's over.
She valued not what others thought her,
And was— his most obedient daughter.'
Fair maidens all, attend the Muse,
Who now the wand'ring pair pursues:
Away they rode in homely sort,
Their journey long, their money short;
The loving couple well bemir'd;
The horse and both the riders tir'd:
Their victuals bad, their lodgings worse;
Phyl cried! and John began to curse:
Phyl wish'd that she had strain'd a limb,
When first she ventured out with him;
John wish'd that he had broke a leg,
When first for her he quitted Peg.

But what adventures more befell 'em,
The Muse hath now no time to tell 'em;
How Johnny wheedled, threaten'd, fawn'd,
Till Phyllis all her trinkets pawn'd:
How oft she broke her marriage vows,
In kindness to maintain her spouse,
Till swains unwholesome spoil'd the trade;
For now the surgeon must be paid,
To whom those perquisites are gone,
In Christian justice due to John.

When food and raiment now grew scarce,
Fate put a period to the farce,
And with exact poetic justice;
For John was landlord, Phyllis hostess;
They keep, at Stains, the Old Blue Boar,
Are cat and dog, and rogue and whore.

ADVICE
To the Grub-Street Verse-Writers

Ye poets ragged and forlorn,
    Down from your garrets haste;
Ye rhymers, dead as soon as born,
    Not yet consign'd to paste;

I know a trick to make you thrive;
    O, 'tis a quaint device:
Your still-born poems shall revive,
    And scorn to wrap up spice.

Get all your verses printed fair,
    Then let them well be dried;
And Curll must have a special care
    To leave the margin wide.

Lend these to paper-sparing Pope;
    And when he sets to write,
No letter with an envelope
    Could give him more delight.

When Pope has fill'd the margins round,
    Why then recall your loan;
Sell them to Curll for fifty pound,
    And swear they are your own.

DESIRE AND POSSESSION

'Tis strange what different thoughts inspire
In men, Possession and Desire!
Think what they wish so great a blessing;
So disappointed when possessing!
    A moralist profoundly sage
(I know not in what book or page,
Or whether o'er a pot of ale)
Related thus the following tale.
    Possession, and Desire, his brother,
But still at variance with each other,
Were seen contending in a race;
And kept at first an equal pace;
'Tis said, their course continued long,
For this was active, that was strong:
Till Envy, Slander, Sloth and Doubt,
Misled them many a league about;
Seduced by some deceiving light,
They take the wrong way for the right;
Through slippery by-roads, dark and deep,
They often climb, and often creep.
    Desire, the swifter of the two,
Along the plain like lightning flew:
Till, entering on a broad highway,
Where power and titles scatter'd lay,
He strove to pick up all he found,
And by excursions lost his ground:
No sooner got, than with disdain
He threw them on the ground again;
And hastened forward to pursue
Fresh objects, fairer to his view,
In hope to spring some nobler game;
But all he took was just the same:
Too scornful now to stop his pace,

26

He spurn'd them in his rival's face.

    Possession kept the beaten road,
And gather'd all his brother strew'd;
But overcharged, and out of wind,
Though strong in limbs, he lagg'd behind.

    Desire had now the goal in sight;
It was a tower of monstrous height;
Where on the summit Fortune stands,
A crown and sceptre in her hands;
Beneath, a chasm as deep as Hell,
Where many a bold adventurer fell.
Desire, in rapture, gazed awhile,
And saw the treacherous goddess smile.
But as he climb'd to grasp the crown,
She knock'd him with the sceptre down!
He tumbled in the gulf profound;
There doom'd to whirl an endless round.

    Possession's load was grown so great,
He sunk beneath the cumbrous weight;
And, as he now expiring lay,
Flocks every ominous bird of prey;
The raven, vulture, owl and kite;
At once upon his carcass light,
And strip his hide, and pick his bones,
Regardless of his dying groans.

CLEVER TOM CLINCH
Going to be Hanged, 1727

As clever Tom Clinch, while the rabble was bawling,
Rode stately through Holborn to die in his calling,
He stopt at the George for a bottle of sack,
And promised to pay for it when he came back.

His waistcoat, and stockings, and breeches, were white;
His cap had a new cherry ribbon to tie't.
The maids to the doors and the balconies ran,
And said, 'Lack-a-day, he's a proper young man!'
But, as from the windows the ladies he spied,
Like a beau in the box, he bow'd low on each side!
And when his last speech the loud hawkers did cry,
He swore from his cart, 'It was all a damn'd lie!'
The hangman for pardon fell down on his knee;
Tom gave him a kick in the guts for his fee:
Then said, 'I must speak to the people a little;
But I'll see you all damn'd before I will whittle.
My honest friend Wild (may he long hold his place)
He lengthen'd my life with a whole year of grace.
Take courage, dear comrades, and be not afraid,
Nor slip this occasion to follow your trade;
My conscience is clear, and my spirits are calm,
And thus I go off, without prayer-book or psalm;
Then follow the practice of clever Tom Clinch,
Who hung like a hero, and never would flinch.'

DR. SWIFT TO MR. POPE
While he was writing the Dunciad, 1727

Pope has the talent well to speak,
   But not to reach the ear;
His loudest voice is low and weak,
   The Dean too deaf to hear.

Awhile they on each other look,
   Then different studies choose;
The Dean sits plodding on a book;
   Pope walks, and courts the Muse.

Now backs of letters, though design'd
   For those who more will need 'em,
Are fill'd with hints, and interlined
   Himself can hardly read 'em.

Each atom by some other struck
   All turns and motions tries;
Till in a lump together stuck,
   Behold a poem rise:

Yet to the Dean his share allot;
   He claims it by a canon;
That without which a thing is not,
   Is *causa sine qua non*.

Thus, Pope, in vain you boast your wit;
   For, had our deaf divine
Been for your conversation fit,
   You had not writ a line.

Of Sherlock, thus, for preaching framed
   The sexton reason'd well;
And justly half the merit claim'd,
   Because he rang the bell.

THE POWER OF TIME

If neither brass nor marble can withstand
The mortal force of Time's destructive hand;
If mountains sink to vales, if cities die,
And lessening rivers mourn their fountains dry;
When my old cassock (said a Welsh divine)
Is out at elbows, why should I repine?

THE DAY OF JUDGMENT

With a whirl of thought oppress'd,
I sunk from reverie to rest.
An horrid vision seized my head;
I saw the graves give up their dead!
Jove, arm'd with terrors, bursts the skies,
And thunder roars and lightning flies!
Amaz'd, confus'd, its fate unknown,
The world stands trembling at his throne!
While each pale sinner hung his head,
Jove, nodding, shook the heavens, and said:
'Offending race of human kind,
By nature, reason, *learning*, blind;
You who, through frailty, stepp'd aside;
And you, who never fell—*through pride:*
You who in different sects were shamm'd,
And come to see each other damn'd;
(So some folk told you, but they knew
No more of Jove's designs than you;)
—The world's mad business now is o'er,
And I resent these pranks no more.
—I to such blockheads set my wit!
I damn such fools!—Go, go, you're *bit.*'

from
ON THE DEATH OF DR. SWIFT

The time is not remote, when I
Must by the course of nature die;
When, I foresee, my special friends
Will try to find their private ends:
Tho' it is hardly understood
Which way my death can do them good,

Yet thus, methinks, I hear 'em speak:
'See, how the Dean begins to break!
Poor gentleman, he droops apace!
You plainly find it in his face.
That old vertigo in his head
Will never leave him till he's dead.
Besides, his memory decays:
He recollects not what he says;
He cannot call his friends to mind:
Forgets the place where last he din'd;
Plyes you with stories o'er and o'er;
He told them fifty times before.
How does he fancy we can sit
To hear his out-of-fashion wit?
But he takes up with younger folks,
Who for his wine will bear his jokes.
Faith! he must make his stories shorter,
Or change his comrades once a quarter:
In half the time he talks them round,
There must another set be found.

  'For poetry he's past his prime:
He takes an hour to find a rhyme;
His fire is out, his wit decay'd,
His fancy sunk, his Muse a jade.
I'd have him throw away his pen;—
But there's no talking to some men!'

  And then their tenderness appears,
By adding largely to my years;
'He's older than he would be reckon'd,
And well remembers Charles the Second.
He hardly drinks a pint of wine;
And that, I doubt, is no good sign.
His stomach too begins to fail:
Last year we thought him strong and hale;
But now he's quite another thing:

I wish he may hold out till spring!'
Then hug themselves, and reason thus:
'It is not yet so bad with us!'

     *   *   *

  Behold the fatal day arrive!
'How is the Dean?'—'He's just alive.'
Now the departing prayer is read;
'He hardly breathes.'—'The Dean is dead.'
  Before the Passing-bell begun,
The news thro' half the town has run.
'O! may we all for death prepare!
What has he left? and who's his heir?'—
'I know no more than what the news is;
'Tis all bequeath'd to public uses.'—
'To public use! a perfect whim!
What had the public done for him?
Mere envy, avarice, and pride:
He gave it all—but first he died.
And had the Dean, in all the nation,
No worthy friend, no poor relation?
So ready to do strangers good,
Forgetting his own flesh and blood!'
  Now Grub-Street wits are all employ'd;
With elegies the town is cloy'd:
Some paragraph in ev'ry paper
To curse the Dean, or bless the Drapier.
  The doctors, tender of their fame,
Wisely on me lay all the blame:
'We must confess, his case was nice;
But he would never take advice.
Had he been ruled for aught appears,
He might have lived these twenty years;
For, when we open'd him, we found,
That all his vital parts were sound.'

From Dublin soon to London spread,
'Tis told at court, 'The Dean is dead.'
Kind Lady Suffolk, in the spleen,
Runs laughing up to tell the queen.
The queen, so gracious, mild and good,
Cries, 'Is he gone! 'tis time he shou'd.
He's dead, you say; why, let him rot:
I'm glad the medals were forgot.
I promised him, I own; but when?
I only was a princess then;
But now, as consort of a king,
You know, 'tis quite a different thing.'
Now Chartres, at Sir Robert's levee,
Tells with a sneer the tidings heavy:
'Why, is he dead without his shoes,'
Cries Bob, 'I'm sorry for the news:
O, were the wretch but living still,
And in his place my good friend Will!
Or had a mitre on his head,
Provided Bolingbroke were dead!'
Now Curll his shop from rubbish drains:
Three genuine tomes of Swift's remains!
And then, to make them pass the glibber,
Revised by Tibbalds, Moore and Cibber.
He'll treat me as he does my betters,
Publish my will, my life, my letters:
Revive the libels born to die;
Which Pope must bear, as well as I.

Here shift the scene, to represent
How those I love my death lament.
Poor Pope will grieve a month, and Gay
A week, and Arbuthnot a day.

St. John himself will scarce forbear
To bite his pen, and drop a tear.
The rest will give a shrug, and cry,

'I'm sorry—but we all must die!'
Indifference, clad in Wisdom's guise,
All fortitude of mind supplies:
For how can stony bowels melt
In those who never pity felt!
When *we* are lash'd, *they* kiss the rod,
Resigning to the will of God.

The fools, my juniors by a year,
Are tortur'd with suspense and fear;
Who wisely thought my age a screen,
When death approach'd, to stand between:
The screen removed, their hearts are trembling;
They mourn for me without dissembling.

My female friends, whose tender hearts
Rave better learn'd to act their parts,
Heceive the news in doleful dumps:
'The Dean is dead: (and what is trumps?)
Then, Lord have mercy on his soul!
(Ladies, I'll venture for the vole.)
Six deans, they say, must bear the pall:
(I wish I knew what King to call.)
Madam, your husband will attend
The funeral of so good a friend.
No, madam, 'tis a shocking sight:
And he's engaged to-morrow night:
My Lady Club wou'd take it ill,
If he shou'd fail her at quadrille.
He loved the Dean—(I lead a heart,)
But dearest friends, they say, must part.
His time was come: he ran his race;
We hope he's in a better place.'

Why do we grieve that friends should die?
No loss more easy to supply.
One year is past; a different scene!
No further mention of the Dean;

Who now, alas! no more is miss'd,
Than if he never did exist.
Where's now this fav'rite of Apollo!
Departed:—and his works must follow;
Must undergo the common fate;
His kind of wit is out of date.

Some country squire to Lintot goes,
Inquires for 'Swift in Verse and Prose.'
Says Lintot, 'I have heard the name;
He died a year ago.'—'The same.'
He searches all the shop in vain.
'Sir, you may find them in Duck-lane;
I sent them with a load of books,
Last Monday to the pastry-cook's.
To fancy they could live a year!
I find you're but a stranger here.
The Dean was famous in his time,
And had a kind of knack at rhyme.
His way of writing now is past;
The town has got a better taste;
I keep no antiquated stuff,
But spick and span I have enough.
Pray do but give me leave to show 'em;
Here's Colley Cibber's birth-day poem.
This ode you never yet have seen,
By Stephen Duck, upon the queen.'

*　　*　　*

Suppose me dead; and then suppose
A club assembled at the Rose;
Where, from discourse of this and that,
I grow the subject of their chat.
And while they toss my name about,
With favour some, and some without,
One, quite indiff'rent in the cause,

35

My character impartial draws:
  'The Dean, if we believe report,
Was never ill receiv'd at court.
As for his works in verse and prose
I own myself no judge of those;
Nor can I tell what critics thought 'em:
But this I know, all people bought 'em.
As with a moral view design'd
To cure the vices of mankind:
And, if he often miss'd his aim,
The world must own it, to their shame,
The praise is his, and theirs the blame.
  'Sir, I have heard another story:
He was a most confounded Tory,
And grew, or he is much belied,
Extremely dull, before he died.'
  Can we the Drapier then forget?
Is not our nation in his debt?
'Twas he that writ the Drapiers letters!—
  'He should have left them for his betters,
We had a hundred abler men,
Nor need depend upon his pen.—
Say what you will about his reading,
You never can defend his breeding;
Who in his satires running riot,
Could never leave the world in quiet;
Attacking, when he took the whim,
Court, city, camp—all one to him.—
  'But why should he, except he slobber't,
Offend our patriot, great Sir Robert,
Whose counsels aid the sov'reign power
To save the nation every hour?
What scenes of evil he unravels
In satires, libels, lying travels!
Not sparing his own clergy-cloth,

But eats into it, like a moth!'
His vein, ironically grave,
Exposed the fool, and lash'd the knave.
To steal a hint was never known,
But what he writ was all his own.

   'He never thought an honour done him,
Because a duke was proud to own him,
Would rather slip aside and chuse
To talk with wits in dirty shoes;
Despised the fools with stars and garters,
So often seen caressing Chartres.
He never courted men in station,
Nor persons held in admiration;
Of no man's greatness was afraid,
Because he sought for no man's aid.
Though trusted long in great affairs
He gave himself no haughty airs:
Without regarding private ends,
Spent all his credit for his friends;
And only chose the wise and good;
No flatterers; no allies in blood:
But succour'd virtue in distress,
And seldom fail'd of good success;
As numbers in their hearts must own,
Who, but for him, had been unknown.

*   *   *

'By innocence and resolution,
He bore continual persecution;
While numbers to preferment rose,
Whose merits were, to be his foes;
When *ev'n his own familiar friends,*
Intent upon their private ends,
Like renegadoes now he feels,
Against him lifting up their heels.

37

'The Dean did, by his pen, defeat
An infamous destructive cheat;
Taught fools their int'rest how to know,
And gave them arms to ward the blow.
Envy has own'd it was his doing,
To save that hapless land from ruin;
While they who at the steerage stood,
And reap'd the profit, sought his blood.

*   *   *

'Perhaps I may allow the Dean,
Had too much satire in his vein;
And seem'd determined not to starve it,
Because no age could more deserve it.
Yet malice never was his aim;
He lash'd the vice, but spared the name;
No individual could resent,
Where thousands equally were meant;
His satire points at no defect,
But what all mortals may correct;
For he abhorr'd that senseless tribe
Who call it humour when they gibe:
He spared a hump, or crooked nose,
Whose owners set not up for beaux.
True genuine dulness moved his pity,
Unless it offer'd to be witty.
Those who their ignorance confest,
He ne'er offended with a jest;
But laugh'd to hear an idiot quote
A verse from Horace learn'd by rote.

'Vice, if it e'er can be abash'd,
Must be or ridiculed or lash'd.
If you resent it, who's to blame?
He neither knew you nor your name.
Should vice expect to 'scape rebuke,

Because his owner is a duke?
  'He knew an hundred pleasant stories,
With all the turns of Whigs and Tories:
Was cheerful to his dying day;
And friends would let him have his way.
  'He gave the little wealth he had
To build a house for fools and mad;
And show'd by one satiric touch,
No nation wanted it so much.
That kingdom he hath left his debtor,
I wish it soon may have a better.
And, since you dread no farther lashes
Methinks you may forgive his ashes.'

ON A CURATE'S COMPLAINT OF HARD DUTY

I MARCH'D three miles through scorching sand,
With zeal in heart, and notes in hand;
I rode four more to Great St. Mary,
Using four legs, when two were weary:
To three fair virgins I did tie men,
In the close bands of pleasing Hymen;
I dipp'd two babes in holy water,
And purified their mother after.
Within an hour and eke a half,
I preach'd three congregations deaf;
Where, thundering out, with lungs long-winded,
I chopp'd so fast, that few there minded.
My emblem, the laborious sun,
Saw all these mighty labours done
Before one race of his was run.
All this perform'd by Robert Hewit:
What mortal else could e'er go through it!

EPIGRAM

As Thomas was cudgell'd one day by his wife,
He took to the street, and fled for his life:
Tom's three dearest friends came by in the squabble,
And saved him at once from the shrew and the rabble;
Then ventured to give him some sober advice—
But Tom is a person of honour so nice,
Too wise to take counsel, too proud to take warning,
That he sent to all three a challenge next morning.
Three duels he fought, thrice ventur'd his life;
Went home, and was cudgell'd again by his wife.

from
CADENUS AND VANESSA

Cupid, though all his darts were lost,
Yet still resolved to spare no cost:
He could not answer to his fame
The triumphs of that stubborn dame,
A nymph so hard to be subdued,
Who neither was coquette nor prude.
I find, said he, she wants a doctor,
Both to adore her, and instruct her:
I'll give her what she most admires
Among those venerable sires.
Cadenus is a subject fit,
Grown old in politics and wit,
Caress'd by ministers of state,
Of half mankind the dread and hate.
Whate'er vexations love attend,
She needs no rivals apprehend.
Her sex, with universal voice,
Must laugh at her capricious choice.

Cadenus many things had writ:
Vanessa much esteem'd his wit,
And call'd for his poetic works:
Meantime the boy in secret lurks;
And, while the book was in her hand,
The urchin from his private stand
Took aim, and shot with all his strength
A dart of such prodigious length,
It pierced the feeble volume through,
And deep transfix'd her bosom too.
Some lines, more moving than the rest,
Stuck to the point that pierced her breast,
And, borne directly to the heart,
With pains unknown increased her smart.

Vanessa, not in years a score,
Dreams of a gown of forty-four;
Imaginary charms can find
In eyes with reading almost blind:
Cadenus now no more appears
Declined in health, advanced in years.
She fancies music in his tongue;
Nor farther looks, but thinks him young.
What mariner is not afraid
To venture in a ship decay'd?
What planter will attempt to yoke
A sapling with a falling oak?
As years increase, she brighter shines;
Cadenus with each day declines:
And he must fall a prey to time,
While she continues in her prime.
Cadenus, common forms apart,
In every scene had kept his heart;
Had sigh'd and languish'd, vow'd and writ,
For pastime, or to show his wit,
But books, and time, and state affairs,

Had spoil'd his fashionable airs:
He now could praise, esteem, approve,
But understood not what was love.
His conduct might have made him styled
A father, and the nymph his child.
That innocent delight he took
To see the virgin mind her book,
Was but the master's secret joy
In school to hear the finest boy.
Her knowledge with her fancy grew;
She hourly press'd for something new;
Ideas came into her mind
So fast, his lessons lagg'd behind;
She reason'd, without plodding long,
Nor ever gave her judgment wrong.
But now a sudden change was wrought;
She minds no longer what he taught.
Cadenus was amazed to find
Such marks of a distracted mind:
For, though she seem'd to listen more
To all he spoke, than e'er before,
He found her thoughts would absent range,
Yet guess'd not whence could spring the change.
And first he modestly conjectures
His pupil might be tired with lectures;
Which help'd to mortify his pride,
Yet gave him not the heart to chide:
But, in a mild dejected strain,
At last he ventured to complain:
Said, she should be no longer teazed,
Might have her freedom when she pleased;
Was now convinced he acted wrong
To hide her from the world so long,
And in dull studies to engage
One of her tender sex and age;

That every nymph with envy own'd,
How she might shine in the *grand monde*:
And every shepherd was undone
To see her cloister'd like a nun.
This was a visionary scheme:
He waked, and found it but a dream;
A project far above his skill:
For nature must be nature still.
If he were bolder than became
A scholar to a courtly dame,
She might excuse a man of letters;
Thus tutors often treat their betters;
And, since his talk offensive grew,
He came to take his last adieu.

   Vanessa, fill'd with just disdain,
Would still her dignity maintain,
Instructed from her early years
To scorn the art of female tears.

   Had he employ'd his time so long
To teach her what was right and wrong;
Yet could such notions entertain
That all his lectures were in vain?
She own'd the wandering of her thoughts;
But he must answer for her faults.
She well remember'd to her cost,
That all his lessons were not lost.
Two maxims she could still produce,
And sad experience taught their use;
That virtue, pleased by being shown,
Knows nothing which it dares not own;
Can make us without fear disclose
Our inmost secrets to our foes;
That common forms were not design'd
Directors to a noble mind.
Not, said the nymph, to let you see

My actions with your rules agree;
That I can vulgar forms despise,
And have no secrets to disguise;
I knew, by what you said and writ,
How dangerous things were men of wit;
You caution'd me against their charms,
But never gave me equal arms;
Your lessons found the weakest part,
Aim'd at the head, but reach'd the heart.

   Cadenus felt within him rise
Shame, disappointment, guilt, surprise.
He knew not how to reconcile
Such language with her usual style:
And yet her words were so exprest,
He could not hope she spoke in jest.
His thoughts had wholly been confined
To form and cultivate her mind.
He hardly knew, till he was told,
Whether the nymph were young or old;
Had met her in a public place,
Without distinguishing her face;
Much less could his declining age
Vanessa's earliest thoughts engage;
And, if her youth indifference met,
His person must contempt beget;
Or grant her passion be sincere,
How shall his innocence be clear?
Appearances were all so strong,
The world must think him in the wrong;
Would say, he made a treacherous use
Of wit, to flatter and seduce;
The town would swear, he had betray'd
By magic spells the harmless maid:
And every beau would have his joke,
That scholars were like other folk;

And, when Platonic flights were over,
The tutor turn'd a mortal lover!
So tender of the young and fair!
It show'd a true paternal care—
Five thousand guineas in her purse!
The doctor might have fancied worse.—

    Hardly at length he silence broke,
And falter'd every word he spoke;
Interpreting her complaisance,
Just as a man *sans* consequence.
She rallied well, he always knew:
Her manner now was something new;
And what she spoke was in an air
As serious as a tragic player.
But those who aim at ridicule
Should fix upon some certain rule,
Which fairly hints they are in jest,
Else he must enter his protest:
For let a man be ne'er so wise,
He may be caught with sober lies;
A science which he never taught,
And, to be free, was dearly bought;
For, take it in its proper light,
'Tis just what coxcombs call a bite.

    But, not to dwell on things minute,
Vanessa finish'd the dispute;
Brought weighty arguments to prove
That reason was her guide in love.
She thought he had himself described,
His doctrines when she first imbibed;
What he had planted, now was grown;
His virtues she might call her own;
As he approves, as he dislikes,
Love or contempt her fancy strikes.
Self-love, in nature rooted fast,

Attends us first, and leaves us last;
Why she likes him, admire not at her;
She loves herself, and that's the matter.
How was her tutor wont to praise
The geniuses of ancient days!
(Those authors he so oft had named,
For learning, wit, and wisdom, famed;)
Was struck with love, esteem, and awe
For persons whom he never saw.
Suppose Cadenus flourish'd then,
He must adore such godlike men.
If one short volume could comprise
All that was witty, learn'd, and wise,
How would it be esteem'd and read,
Although the writer long were dead!
If such an author were alive,
How all would for his friendship strive,
And come in crowds to see his face!
And this she takes to be her case.
Cadenus answers every end,
The book, the author, and the friend;
The utmost her desires will reach,
Is but to learn what he can teach:
His converse is a system fit
Alone to fill up all her wit;
While every passion of her mind
In him is centred and confined.

Love can with speech inspire a mute,
And taught Vanessa to dispute.
This topic, never touch'd before,
Display'd her eloquence the more:
Her knowledge, with such pains acquired,
By this new passion grew inspired;
Through this she made all objects pass,
Which gave a tincture o'er the mass;

As rivers, though they bend and twine,
Still to the sea their course incline:
Or, as philosophers, who find
Some favourite system to their mind;
In every point to make it fit,
Will force all nature to submit.
   Cadenus, who could ne'er suspect
His lessons would have such effect,
Or be so artfully applied,
Insensibly came on her side.
It was an unforeseen event;
Things took a turn he never meant.
Whoe'er excels in what we prize,
Appears a hero in our eyes;
Each girl, when pleased with what is taught,
Will have the teacher in her thought.
When miss delights in her spinet,
A fiddler may a fortune get;
A blockhead, with melodious voice,
In boarding-schools may have his choice:
And oft the dancing-master's art
Climbs from the toe to touch the heart.
In learning let a nymph delight,
The pedant gets a mistress by't.
Cadenus, to his grief and shame,
Could scarce oppose Vanessa's flame;
And, though her arguments were strong,
At least could hardly wish them wrong.
Howe'er it came, he could not tell,
But sure she never talk'd so well.
His pride began to interpose;
Preferr'd before a crowd of beaux!
So bright a nymph to come unsought!
Such wonder by his merit wrought!
'Tis merit must with her prevail!

He never knew her judgment fail!
She noted all she ever read!
And had a most discerning head!
   'Tis an old maxim in the schools,
That flattery's the food of fools;
Yet now and then your men of wit
Will condescend to take a bit.
   So when Cadenus could not hide,
He chose to justify his pride;
Construing the passion she had shown,
Much to her praise, more to his own.
Nature in him had merit placed,
In her a most judicious taste.
Love, hitherto a transient guest,
Ne'er held possession of his breast;
So long attending at the gate,
Disdain'd to enter in so late.
Love why do we one passion call,
When 'tis a compound of them all?
Where hot and cold, where sharp and sweet,
In all their equipages meet;
Where pleasures mix'd with pains appear,
Sorrow with joy, and hope with fear;
Wherein his dignity and age
Forbid Cadenus to engage.
But friendship, in its greatest height,
A constant, rational delight,
On virtue's basis fix'd to last,
When love's allurements long are past,
Which gently warms, but cannot burn,
He gladly offers in return;
His want of passion will redeem
With gratitude, respect, esteem:
With what devotion we bestow,
When goddesses appear below.

While thus Cadenus entertains
Vanessa in exalted strains,
The nymph in sober words entreats
A truce with all sublime conceits;
For why such raptures, flights, and fancies,
To her who durst not read romances?
In lofty style to make replies,
Which he had taught her to despise?
But when her tutor will affect
Devotion, duty, and respect,
He fairly abdicates the throne:
The government is now her own;
He has a forfeiture incurr'd;
She vows to take him at his word,
And hopes he will not think it strange,
If both should now their stations change,
The nymph will have her turn to be
The tutor; and the pupil, he;
Though she already can discern
Her scholar is not apt to learn;
Or wants capacity to reach
The science she designs to teach;
Wherein his genius was below
The skill of every common beau,
Who, though he cannot spell, is wise
Enough to read a lady's eyes,
And will each accidental glance
Interpret for a kind advance.
But what success Vanessa met,
Is to the world a secret yet.
Whether the nymph, to please her swain,
Talks in a high romantic strain;
Or whether he at last descends
To act with less seraphic ends;

Or to compound the business, whether
They temper love and books together;
Must never to mankind be told,
Nor shall the conscious Muse unfold.

STELLA'S BIRTH-DAY
13 March 1718–19

STELLA this day is thirty-four,
(We shan't dispute a year or more:)
However, Stella, be not troubled,
Although thy size and years are doubled
Since first I saw thee at sixteen,
The brightest virgin on the green;
So little is thy form declined;
Made up so largely in thy mind.
   O, would it please the gods to split
Thy beauty, size, and years, and wit!
No age could furnish out a pair
Of nymphs so graceful, wise, and fair,
With half the lustre of your eyes,
With half your wit, your years, and size.
And then, before it grew too late,
How should I beg of gentle fate,
(That either nymph might have her swain,)
To split my worship too in twain.

TO STELLA
On her Birth-day, 1721–2

WHILE, Stella, to your lasting praise
The Muse her annual tribute pays,
While I assign myself a task
Which you expect, but scorn to ask;
If I perform this task with pain,
Let me of partial fate complain;
You every year the debt enlarge,
I grow less equal to the charge:
In you each virtue brighter shines,
But my poetic vein declines;
My harp will soon in vain be strung,
And all your virtues left unsung.
For none among the upstart race
Of poets dare assume my place;
Your worth will be to them unknown,
They must have Stellas of their own;
And thus, my stock of wit decay'd,
I dying leave the debt unpaid,
Unless Delany, as my heir,
Will answer for the whole arrear.

TO STELLA
Written on the day of her Birth, 13 March 1723–4, but not on the subject, When I was Sick in Bed

TORMENTED with incessant pains,
Can I devise poetic strains?
Time was, when I could yearly pay
My verse to Stella's native day:

But now unable grown to write,
I grieve she ever saw the light.
Ungrateful! since to her I owe
That I these pains can undergo.
She tends me like an humble slave;
And, when indecently I rave,
When out my brutish passions break,
With gall in every word I speak,
She with soft speech my anguish cheers,
Or melts my passions down with tears;
Although 'tis easy to descry
She wants assistance more than I;
Yet seems to feel my pains alone,
And is a stoic in her own.
When, among scholars, can we find
So soft and yet so firm a mind?
All accidents of life conspire
To raise up Stella's virtue higher;
Or else to introduce the rest
Which had been latent in her breast.
Her firmness who could e'er have known,
Had she not evils of her own?
Her kindness who could ever guess,
Had not her friends been in distress?
Whatever base returns you find
From me, dear Stella, still be kind.
In your own heart you'll reap the fruit,
Though I continue still a brute.
But, when I once am out of pain,
I promise to be good again;
Meantime, your other juster friends
Shall for my follies make amends;
So may we long continue thus,
Admiring you, you pitying us.

As, when a beautious nymph decays,
We say she's past her dancing days;
So poets lose their feet by time,
And can no longer dance in rhyme.
Your annual bard had rather chose
To celebrate your birth in prose:
Yet merry folks, who want by chance
A pair to make a country dance,
Call the old housekeeper, and get her
To fill a place for want of better:
While Sheridan is off the hooks,
And friend Delany at his books,
That Stella may avoid disgrace,
Once more the Dean supplies their place.

    Beauty and wit, too sad a truth!
Have always been confined to youth;
The god of wit and beauty's queen,
He twenty-one and she fifteen,
No poet ever sweetly sung,
Unless he were, like Phœbus, young;
Nor ever nymph inspired to rhyme,
Unless, like Venus, in her prime.
At fifty-six, if this be true,
Am I a poet fit for you?
Or, at the age of forty-three,
Are you a subject fit for me?
Adieu! bright wit, and radiant eyes!
You must be grave and I be wise.
Our fate in vain we would oppose:
But I'll be still your friend in prose:
Esteem and friendship to express,
Will not require poetic dress;

And if the Muse deny her aid
To have them sung, they may be said.
   But, Stella, say, what evil tongue
Reports you are no longer young;
That Time sits with his scythe to mow
Where erst sat Cupid with his bow;
That half your locks are turn'd to gray?
I'll ne'er believe a word they say.
'Tis true, but let it not be known,
My eyes are somewhat dimmish grown;
For nature, always in the right,
To your decays adapts my sight;
And wrinkles undistinguish'd pass,
For I'm ashamed to use a glass:
And till I see them with these eyes,
Whoever says you have them, lies.
No length of time can make you quit
Honour and virtue, sense and wit;
Thus you may still be young to me,
While I can better hear than see.
O ne'er may Fortune show her spite,
To make me deaf, and mend my sight!

ON THE COLLAR OF TIGER
Mrs. Dingley's Lap-Dog

PRAY steal me not; I'm Mrs. Dingley's,
Whose heart in this four-footed thing lies.

STELLA'S BIRTH-DAY,
13 March 1726-7

This day, whate'er the Fates decree,
Shall still be kept with joy by me:
This day then let us not be told,
That you are sick, and I grown old;
Nor think on our approaching ills,
And talk of spectacles and pills;
To-morrow will be time enough
To hear such mortifying stuff.
Yet, since from reason may be brought
A better and more pleasing thought,
Which can, in spite of all decays,
Support a few remaining days;
From not the gravest of divines
Accept for once some serious lines.

Although we now can form no more
Long schemes of life, as heretofore;
Yet you, while time is running fast,
Can look with joy on what is past.

Were future happiness and pain
A mere contrivance of the brain;
As atheists argue, to entice
And fit their proselytes for vice;
(The only comfort they propose,
To have companions in their woes;)
Grant this the case; yet sure 'tis hard
That virtue, styled its own reward,
And by all sages understood
To be the chief of human good,
Should acting die; nor leave behind
Some lasting pleasure in the mind,
Which, by remembrance will assuage
Grief, sickness, poverty, and age;

And strongly shoot a radiant dart
To shine through life's declining part.
    Say, Stella, feel you no content,
Reflecting on a life well spent?
Your skilful hand employ'd to save
Despairing wretches from the grave;
And then supporting with your store
Those whom you dragg'd from death before?
So Providence on mortals waits,
Preserving what it first creates.
Your generous boldness to defend
An innocent and absent friend;
That courage which can make you just
To merit humbled in the dust;
The detestation you express
For vice in all its glittering dress;
That patience under torturing pain,
Where stubborn stoics would complain:
Must these like empty shadows pass,
Or forms reflected from a glass?
Or mere chimeras in the mind,
That fly, and leave no marks behind?
Does not the body thrive and grow
By food of twenty years ago?
And, had it not been still supplied,
It must a thousand times have died.
Then who with reason can maintain
That no effects of food remain?
And is not virtue in mankind
The nutriment that feeds the mind;
Upheld by each good action past,
And still continued by the last?
Then, who with reason can pretend
That all effects of virtue end?
    Believe me, Stella, when you show

That true contempt for things below,
Nor prize your life for other ends,
Than merely to oblige your friends;
Your former actions claim their part,
And join to fortify your heart.
For Virtue, in her daily race,
Like Janus, bears a double face;
Looks back with joy where she has gone
And therefore goes with courage on:
She at your sickly couch will wait,
And guide you to a better state.

   O then, whatever Heaven intends,
Take pity on your pitying friends!
Nor let your ills affect your mind,
To fancy they can be unkind.
Me, surely me, you ought to spare,
Who gladly would your suffering share;
Or give my scrap of life to you,
And think it far beneath your due;
You, to whose care so oft I owe
That I'm alive to tell you so.

ON A CORKSCREW

THOUGH I, alas! a prisoner be,
My trade is prisoners to set free.
No slave his lord's commands obeys
With such insinuating ways.
My genius piercing, sharp, and bright,
Wherein the men of wit delight.
The clergy keep me for their ease,
And turn and wind me as they please.
A new and wondrous art I show

Of raising spirits from below;
In scarlet some, and some in white;
They rise, walk round, yet never fright.
In at each mouth the spirits pass,
Distinctly seen as through a glass:
O'er head and body make a rout,
And drive at last all secrets out;
And still, the more I show my art,
The more they open every heart.

A greater chemist none than I
Who, from materials hard and dry,
Have taught men to extract with skill
More precious juice than from a still.

Although I'm often out of case,
I'm not ashamed to show my face.
Though at the tables of the great
I near the sideboard take my seat;
Yet the plain 'squire, when dinner's done,
Is never pleased till I make one;
He kindly bids me near him stand,
And often takes me by the hand.

I twice a-day a-hunting go;
Nor ever fail to seize my foe;
And when I have him by the poll,
I drag him upwards from his hole;
Though some are of so stubborn kind,
I'm forced to leave a limb behind.

I hourly wait some fatal end;
For I can break, but scorn to bend.

ON THE GALLOWS

THERE is a gate, we know full well,
That stands 'twixt Heaven, and Earth, and Hell,
Where many for a passage venture,
Yet very few are fond to enter:
Although 'tis open night and day,
They for that reason shun this way:
Both dukes and lords abhor its wood,
They can't come near it for their blood.
What other way they take to go,
Another time I'll let you know.
Yet commoners with greatest ease
Can find an entrance when they please.
The poorest hither march in state
(Or they can never pass the gate)
Like Roman generals triumphant,
And then they take a turn and jump on't,
If gravest parsons here advance,
They cannot pass before they dance;
There's not a soul that does resort here,
But strips himself to pay the porter.

IN SICKNESS
Written in October 1714
(*Soon after the author's coming to live in Ireland, upon the Queen's death.—Swift.*)

'TIS true—then why should I repine
To see my life so fast decline?
But why obscurely here alone,
Where I am neither loved nor known?
My state of health none care to learn;

My life is here no soul's concern:
And those with whom I now converse
Without a tear will tend my hearse.
Removed from kind Arbuthnot's aid,
Who knows his art, but not his trade,
Preferring his regard for me
Before his credit, or his fee.
Some formal visits, looks, and words,
What mere humanity affords,
I meet perhaps from three or four,
From whom I once expected more;
Which those who tend the sick for pay,
Can act as decently as they:
But no obliging, tender friend,
To help at my approaching end.
My life is now a burthen grown
To others, 'ere it be my own.

   Ye formal weepers for the sick,
In your last offices be quick;
And spare my absent friends the grief
To hear, yet give me no relief;
Expired to-day, entomb'd to-morrow,
When known, will save a double sorrow.

LINES
(Written on a Window in the Episcopal Palace at Kilmore)

RESOLVE me this, ye happy dead,
Who've lain some hundred years in bed,
From every persecution free
That in this wretched life we see;
Would ye resume a second birth,
And choose once more to live on earth?

MARY THE COOK-MAID'S LETTER
To Dr. Sheridan, 1723

WELL, if ever I saw such another man since my mother
    bound up my head!
You a gentleman! Marry come up! I wonder where you were
    bred.
I'm sure such words does not become a man of your cloth;
I would not give such language to a dog, faith and troth.
Yes, you call'd my master a knave; fie, Mr. Sheridan! 'tis a
    shame
For a parson who should know better things, to come out with
    such a name.
Knave in your teeth, Mr. Sheridan! 'tis both a shame and a sin;
And the Dean, my master, is an honester man than you and all
    your kin;
He has more goodness in his little finger than you have in your
    whole body;
My master is a personable man, and not a spindle-shank'd
    hoddy doddy.
And now, whereby I find you would fain make an excuse,
Because my master, one day, in anger, call'd you a goose:
Which, and I am sure I have been his servant four years since
    October,
And he never call'd me worse than sweet-heart, drunk or sober:
Not that I know his reverence was ever concern'd to my know-
    ledge,
Though you and your come-rogues keep him out so late in your
    wicked college.
You say you will eat grass on his grave: a Christian eat grass!
Whereby you now confess yourself to be a goose or an ass:
But that's as much as to say, that my master should die before
    ye;
Well, well, that's as God pleases; and I don't believe that's a
    true story;

And so say I told you so, and you may go tell my master; what
  care I?

And I don't care who knows it; 'tis all one to Mary.

Everybody knows that I love to tell truth, and shame the devil;

I am but a poor servant; but I think gentlefolks should be civil.

Besides, you found fault with our victuals one day that you
  was here;

I remember it was on a Tuesday, of all days in the year.

And Saunders, the man, says you are always jesting and
  mocking:

Mary, said he, (one day as I was mending my master's stock-
  ing;)

My master is so fond of that minister that keeps the school—

I thought my master a wise man, but that man makes him a
  fool.

Saunders, said I, I would rather than a quart of ale

He would come into our kitchen, and I would pin a dish-clout
  to his tail.

And now I must go, and get Saunders to direct this letter;

For I write but a sad scrawl; but my sister Marget she writes
  better.

Well, but I must run and make the bed, before my master
  comes from prayers:

And see now, it strikes ten, and I hear him coming up stairs;

Whereof I could say more to your verses, if I could write
  written hand;

And so I remain, in a civil way, your servant to command,

MARY

62

SWIFT'S EPITAPH
In St. Patrick's Cathedral, Dublin

★

HIC DEPOSITUM EST CORPUS

JONATHAN SWIFT, S.T.D.

HUJUS ECCLESIAE CATHEDRALIS

DECANI;

UBI SAEVA INDIGNATIO

ULTERIUS COR LACERARE NEQUIT.

ABI VIATOR

ET IMITARE, SI POTERIS,

STRENUUM PRO VIRILI LIBERTATEM VINDICEM.

OBIIT ANNO 1745

MENSIS OCTOBRIS DIE 19

AETATIS ANNO 78.

BIBLIOGRAPHY

★

The Poetical Works of Jonathan Swift. Ed. S. Mitford, 3 vols. 1833–34, 1853, 1866 (Aldine edn.)

The Poems of Jonathan Swift. Ed. H. Williams, 3 vols. Oxford 1937.

BIOGRAPHY AND CRITICISM

Johnson, Samuel, *Lives of the Poets*, vol. iii, 1781.

Scott, Sir Walter. Memoir (in *The Works of Jonathan Swift*, 1814).

Hazlitt, William, *Lectures on the English Poets*, 1818.

Thackeray, W. M., *The English Humourists of the Eighteenth Century*, 1853.

Craik, Sir Henry, *Life of Jonathan Swift*, 1882.

Stephen, Sir Leslie, *Jonathan Swift*, 1882 (English Men of Letters Series).

Leslie, Shane, *The Skull of Swift*, 1928.

Read, Herbert, 'Swift.' (In *The Sense of Glory*, Cambridge 1929.)

Huxley, Aldous, 'Swift.' (In *Do What You Will*, 1929.)

Van Doren, Carl, *Swift*, 1930.

Gwynn, Stephen, *The Life and Friendships of Dean Swift*, 1933.

Taylor, W. D., *Jonathan Swift, a Critical Essay*, 1933.

Johnston, Denis, 'The Mysterious Origin of Dean Swift.' (In *The Dublin Historical Record*, June 1941.)

Davis, Herbert, *Stella, a Gentlewoman of the Eighteenth Century*, New York 1942.